REASONS WHY
WE'RE ANGRY

ALSO BY SOPHIA ISABELLA MURRAY

The Alchemist's Daughter

Reasons Why We're Angry

Sophia Isabella Murray

QUERENCIA

Querencia Press, LLC
Chicago, Illinois

QUERENCIA PRESS

ISBN 978 1 959118 07 7

www.querenciapress.com

First Published in 2022

Querencia Press, LLC
Chicago IL

Printed & Bound in the United States of America

To K, who taught me grace.

CONTENTS

I Have Yet to Learn to Love

Dear girl standing on the stairs I'm afraid to look at,

long rat tails hanging either side of a rosebud mouth / painted on
snail shell skin so thin / blue vein burrowed above an eyebrow
arched in constant consternation / the cancer of the child within
sitting deep / things confronted in the dim lit stair well

- I'm only here to brush the filth away from an ever
  languishing day

bleary eyed curses in the dark / perpetual itch beneath reptilian skin
moulded in this shape of woman / ever growing you unfurl with me
but not through me / unseen midnight dreams of who we once could
have been/ will be / once were / when you were me

- Even in the light I feel you

growing pains never end / beyond the tidal moon pulled me to shore
/ you at sea bound in ribbons round pigtails the others sneer at /
rough edged puzzle piece that would never fit / jagged edges still
pushed between my ribs

- If only I knew then what I know now

past my nose looking down / reaching in the quiet hours /
remembering a spent book of matches / in tired arms yet to bloom /
one day I'll hold you

Mother/Lode/Stone

stacked on shores
of shale skating
held on skin
burdening the body

bone mother with
scrimshawed histories in
lamplight black
chasing shadows

abhorrent envy of the
hidden self under
charcoal balm to
protect the child

envy of the ravens
even they
are capable
of rational thought

The Cuckoo Song is a Fanfare of Lies

On milk skin
In lemon juice ink
Fountain tip fingernails
Write a little white lie
Painless fiction
Gathers eagerly
The paradox
Of less is more
All I said was…
All I did was…
Your radioactive embrace
Spoils the unseen
Taken in ink
On fresh meat
You remember my
Secrets in black and white
Tattooed on your tongue
Regurgitated readily
We share the decay

Still no answers

I walked to the end of the world

And asked the sun
Saw he was cruel
Selfish with his time

Turned to the moon
Saw she was vain
Sly with the calendar

Asked the stars
And was given a knife
Without any instructions

I suppose they thought I already knew
How to carve the key from a useless bone

Fallow

Labouring the birth of an idea
to cause destruction
Tortured, keening, mistakenly
grieving for a dream
Fallow Constables
landscapes sun faded, arid
left too long to hang
in one place

Waking Up

Awoken again by birdsong, lilac magic threatens to
draw us into this mundane life that no ritual can cleanse
because here we fucking go again. I mean, 'good morning'.

Everything Makes me Anxious

I vibrate with tension every time I click 'join call' in case I'm not on mute or god forbid the camera catches my resting bitch face and double chins holding onto crumbs from hurried toast is revealed for Elaine from accounting to make some slick putdown on a hidden chat. The butterflies death rattle dive in my chest at the thought of being just one minute late to the meeting even it's optional. I feel my soul shrink when I pass a casual acquaintance because I might not remember the name of their third cousin's ex-wife's dogs who died quite recently because a notification on an app told me so. I cringe and crinkle my eyes in fear of looking at a ringing phone in case caller ID is known or unknown and I've forgotten my own name again. A little part of me dies when I get to the self service check out and I say thank you to the machine when it spits out my receipt. My heart shrinks when I'm in a building with glass doors and I might just walk into one again and apologise to my own bruised reflection. My stomach flips when I'm waiting for you in the car park to pick me up and you have forgotten me forever. I lose my breath when your phone pings and it might be her again.

Piano keys after Sylvia Plath's Fig Tree

I saw my life on the ivories / clear cut monochrome keys / playing each singularly with such clarity / moving up with ease / hands drop to C / three white keys / the easy choices with no confrontation / hanging back in an argument / to the accompaniment of bitter drums / triads of minor chords play for days / swaddled in bed / like a helpless newborn / frightened to upset the rhythm / switching to inky flats in staccato / building tension for flight or fight / reaching a riot to make it out alive / to major fifths played fortissimo / reaching a crescendo / of all the right notes / in the wrong order

We Are Agape

we are aligned / light and darkness / the precipice we hang over /
garlands around your neck / my fingers hold / the cut of your jaw /
flourishes of roses on the backs of my hands

in prayer words fail me / mouth open / iron pennies / buds on my
tongue / savouring this body / swept in broken glass / escaping
frames from holy places / we are free

in love / the treasure of this breath / songs in open graves / baptised
in the swell of tides / mother and sunshine in the earth / barefoot
roots blessed with life / we are divine

Avoidance Speech

I wasn't allowed to say your name
I made my own for you

The syllables trip over my tongue
Falling into my chest

An open wound waits for them
A ravenous animal

Consumes each one
In the scrawling script my

Teeth ~~penned~~ could print
The past is mute

Jaws ~~clenched~~ slam together
Teeth a portcullis

Holding back the case
I fill it with earth and spit

~~Now sealed~~ I seal it
~~Each seed~~

Watering with every swallow
New words come for you

Protector
Witness
Aide
I live only in this moment

Loss and Grief (Perte et Deuil)

Under Mount Gabrielle
lives a house of violence
house to house
every home
where were you?
where were you?
ça lui faisait peur
and she felt terrible fear
at this place on the lake

a woman died here
and we all felt responsible
crawling through ideas
making them others
the blow ins
the locals
this place is full of rumour

I remember the last conversation we had
qu'est-ce qu'elle voulait me dire

You did it
You did it
tu l'as fait
tu l'as fait

I went for a walk on St Stephen's Day
saw a fire burning
a deliberate act
released
There was so much more to her
il y avait pour elle tellement plus

How Much of Your Mother Do You Carry With Yourself?

this bothers me most / crawling its way into my tired
consciousness as I try and find unconsciousness at 3am / I was an
egg in my mother while she grew in her mother / how can three
generations of women be so different? / how can they all have
been one? / how did we breathe and live and feed? / did we all
listen to Frank Sinatra / in deep, hot water that spills over the
bathtub / until our skin is pink and raw / craving something salty
never sweet / did we all rebel against the expectations that fathers
held for their perfect daughters? / did we all make bad choices and
suffer the consequences in empty rooms where others avoided us?
/ did we ever all get along? / I was an egg in my mother in her
mother / she carried her who carried me

What She Could Do (If She Weren't Always Told What to Do)

if the clothes she wore were her choice alone to make; if the seat in
the lecture hall was still hers to sit at; if the drivers weren't scared to
take her places without fear of retribution; if the fob to work still let
her in to earn her own living; if the pictures of her face were not
slathered in black paint as if she never existed; if home weren't a
prison and she could walk free without a man beside her; if she
could marry anyone or no one at all; if the images on the salon where
her nails were painted were not whitewashed overnight; if those in
charge had not fled and let her city burn; if the morning songs in
school to learn new things were not muted for fear the men would
hear; if she could sleep knowing her children were safe for one more
day; if the world stopped watching; if the world did something

This Means Anything but Sexual Congress

you stream through synapses in
lavender coils
from the lizard brain
my newly formed tongue
spits you out in hissing rage

delicious force
teeth biting the bottom lip
to feel the 'f' build
to awaken my tribute
and throw out the 'uck'

tongue hits the roof of my mouth
bruised with disdain

Russian Doll

I chip away enamel paint with a fingernail / polka dots caught in the bed / pulled out with another nail in a clean swipe / still there is the force of absence lingering there / constant chipping and scraping / scratching the existential itch / to find the something I'm searching for / does anything lie beneath the lies I'm dressed in? / there is a lost cause hidden / maybe beneath these gaudy layers / another one is peeled away / I am left with splinters in my hands and still no answers / bloodless pastels give way / tender skin not easily forgiven / what I'm missing has been forgotten / with each part of me disrobed in search for nothing / left empty handed / longing with nothing to long for

All the women in me are tired
after Nayyirah Waheed

We are quiet now
tired of the shouting
clipped tones thrown
from the dark place
in our throat
holding space for
everyone else
above our breasts

tense shoulder blades
carrying the weight of
everybody
we hang silently on
hooks at the door
chipping away
never ending lists on the
walls we cling to

curled on the floor in the
way we were and
always will be
behind closed doors
tired
the wolf
the whore
the mother
the healer
the seeker
the leader
and the child
in the arms of each other
sleep

*previously published in Hyacinth Review

On meeting death

God. I said no.
If all she is is good, then where is the joy?
To be good is a straight, unerring line across the desert.
Whipped into shapes only seen from satellites.

Devil. My good lady. I said no.
If all she is is sin, then how is the state of her heart in this breath?
To be laden with sorrow is a hand without feeling,
stuck in an open palm pushing love away.

Death. My friend. I said yes.
If all she sees is the end, then good and evil
cancel one another out and she lives in peace.
Watching the dark spots on the fruit,
they spoil in the basket until she picks the pips,
takes them with her. Life springs from your lips.

IAM(other)

In my otherness I hold this label
Mother knows all the answers
We defied god for knowledge
A bittersweet fruit we nurture and feed

Mother knows all the acts
Referring to our otherness in third person
A bittersweet fruit we nurture and feed
Others calling out mother for what they need

Referring to our otherness in third person
Participants playing in this act of worship
Others calling out mother for what they need
Of this apparent benevolent, omniscient being

Participants playing in this act of worship
Ignorant of mother's other needs
Of this apparent, omniscient being
Sacrificing time, self, energy

Ignorant of mother's other needs
Mother knows all the answers
Sacrificing time, self, energy
In my otherness I hold this label

I am not yet extinct

that first inhale of nicotine in an unlit room; the stretch with morning
strength that sends goosebumps down warm skin; the tepid fresh
coffee with too much milk downed in one thirsty swallow; the XXXL
jumper pulled over unkempt hair hanging to my knees, sleeves
rolled to elbows for anxious hands to begin; the quiet walk in
doorstep woods with the wind our only company; the peanut butter
melting into hot toasted white bread, each bite sticking to the roof of
my mouth and washed down with more coffee, hot this time, sipped
slowly in ritual; The call of 'mum' from other rooms with excited
chatter of the dreams they had, the monsters fought, the places
we've never seen before; the flow of visions you bring to secret
ambitions of a life lived with no soul within 10 miles of where we
hang our hearts; the clatter of pans, the hum of the fan, while you
dance around the kitchen with little ones helping to stir the pot, lay
the table, tasting as they go; The peace after bedtime with only the
quiet turning of the pages of a book disrupting silence; the fresh
linen on our bed with your head next to mine with bright blue eyes
searching my face with a knowing smile; the touch of your hands on
my spine exploring under your T-shirt I stole to sleep in; the lights
out, covers pulled, whisper of 'I love you' before sleep takes you.

When I Ask Myself Questions I Get Answers I Don't Need

If you keep your eyes open for long enough, what do you see?

All that's left inside. A black hole wound that will never heal.

What if you could hold stars in your hands?

I would drop molten silver tears on blackened ribs that crack into electric blue sparks.

What do they taste like?

Lies taste like tangerines. Sweet and sticky that stick to the roof of your mouth peeling ghostly skin from flesh—bitter and unwanted.

On the roof of the world, what do you hear?

The path to god is lined with peonies. You already walk this way.

Spell for Cleansing

wait until the onion skin moon peels itself into shadow. take yourself
to water. envelop your body in the darkness and pull your hands
over goosebump skin to the depths of the riverbed and gather the
silt. carry it to the edge and mould her features in the wet mud, the
hooded eyes, aquiline nose and thin-lipped snarl that whispered you
were no daughter of hers. gather the dead. build around your mired
effigy a circle of nature no more. bring to it the flame you hold in
your hands that weighed so much behind your heart. while fire
crawls black, amber, yellow, usher in the words you could never say
to the face of your mother. spit out the red inked curse. take the
brute force of the energy that lived within you since you felt your
heart break in two and let it travel to your fingertips. rub them into
each palm. let the strength swell until it hurts then release. flatten,
ravage, maim her darkness, her grimy, dirty countenance. smother
the flames and let lilac smoke swaddle you. let it carry you home

Afterword

A few months ago, I told my therapist, without hesitation, that I don't get angry. She looked at me incredulously, which I am not sure therapists are meant to do, and asked—rather obviously for a therapist—why? By the end of a fifty-five-minute session, I was furious. All of the rage, a white-hot magma, crawled its way around the back of my neck and sat heavy on my rib cage. I had pretended to not be angry for 12 years. I had thought it unbecoming of a woman and a mother; a terrible inheritance of 'how we should behave' gifted from a patriarchal society. Once I began to acknowledge it, I reveled in feeling angry. And, dear reader, there is a lot to be angry about, but don't be fooled into thinking that it is an impotent emotion. So much can be done with the fire of that feeling. At the time of writing, women are slowly being stripped of their autonomy, their right to decide what to do with their body, how to behave according to religious doctrine, and as always, trying to find a way to get back home safely. We are fucking furious and rightly so. Anger is the Bunsen burner in the chemical reaction that we need to promote change. It is the palpable energy of our allies marching, writing, speaking, sharing that allows the world to see that we will not take this lying down. If there was ever a time to be angry, this is it.

I am forever grateful to Emily and Querencia Press for publishing my work and for providing invaluable feedback and care with my words. Thank you.